D0911315

Gallery Books
Editor: Peter Fallon

MY SCANDALOUS LIFE

Thomas Kilroy

MY
SCANDALOUS
LIFE

Gallery Books

My Scandalous Life
is first published
simultaneously in paperback
and in a clothbound edition
on 14 December 2004.

The Gallery Press
Loughcrew
Oldcastle
County Meath
Ireland

ISBN 1 85235 378 3 *paperback*
     1 85235 379 1 *clothbound*

A CIP catalogue record for this book
is available from the British Library.

Characters

LORD ALFRED DOUGLAS

Non-speaking
RAYMOND, his son
EILEEN, an Irish maid

Time and Place

The play is set in Hove, England, in 1944. Douglas is aged seventy-four, and it is the year before his death.

Out of the darkness the voice of DOUGLAS, *old and quavering, singing Bach's 'Jesu, Joy of Man's Desiring'.*

'Jesu, joy of man's desiring,
Holy wisdom, Love most bright,
Drawn by Thee our soul's aspiring,
Soar to uncreated light — '

> *Lights on* DOUGLAS *standing, singing, in long dressing gown, cravat and slippers, in the flat of his wife Olive at No 9 Viceroy Lodge, on the seafront at Hove. 1944. He is seventy-four years old, and it is the year before his death. Singing, more tentatively*

'Jesu, joy of man's desiring,
Holy wisdom, Love most bright,
(*Hum*) M-mm-mm-mm-mm-mm-mm — '

> *Night, but, although the curtains are closed, we can see that this is a bright room, blue furnishings and white walls, white glass-doored cupboards of china and glass. A door upstage, centre.* DOUGLAS *turns and peers out into the auditorium.*

Oscar Wilde, did you say? That's all you lot ever ask about. Wilde-Wilde-Wilde-Wilde! For Heaven's sakes, all that was nearly fifty years ago. It's my life now. Why don't you ask about the people who have really mattered in my life? Eh? My darling son, Raymond. My mother. My wife, Olive. Actually she's dying upstairs just now, poor old Olive. That's why I'm here in her flat, you see. Pretty, isn't it? Always had taste, old Olive. Marriage, oho, indeed! We are,

9

of course — what's that word the barristers use? Estranged. That's it. Just could never live together in the same house. Didn't matter in the slightest. She is — (*distressed*) best chum I ever had. Lunched together most weeks. She always had this terrific champagne from Hedges and Butler. Goodies. Best chum. Absolutely. It was love at first sight, you know, Olive and I. Or rather at first sound, because I heard her before I saw her, her voice running prettily up and down the scales before she entered the room. We met as poets and married in the most poetical fashion possible and lived tragically ever after. Oscar was always going on and on about the bloody Greeks but I was the one to experience true tragedy, not he.

Do you know, the very first time I spoke to Olive, the very first thing she said to me was that she didn't care what I had done with Wilde. Sex, you see. Can you imagine that! Said she rather liked fairies, as a matter of fact. Said they always smell so — washed. That's the kind of woman she is. Utterly without cover.

Wrote some tremendously moving sonnets to her, you know. People say some of the finest love sonnets in the language. Since Shakespeare, that is. Mustn't brag. Still. Always say exactly what I mean. Can't abide sneaks.

Would you care to hear some of my poems? No? No? No. I don't suppose this is the appropriate time for that.

Of course our runaway wedding created this fearful rumpus. I was told that King Edward was terribly cross, although what it had to do with him I've never been able to make out. What on earth am I doing, going on with this rubbish! Actually, I think marriage may be one of the most dreadful institutions in human history.

He wanders to the door, opens it, listens, closes it and comes back.

I sat with her earlier up there as she fretted about in the bed, constantly rearranging the bedclothes with her hands, throwing herself about, this way and that. I said to her, Be still, dear! But she wouldn't. Rearing about like a damaged filly.

There'd been another of those damned air-raids, Jerry bombers coming in absurdly low over the rooftops, not in the least frightening, like large grey toys. You could pick out these incredible details, even faces in the cockpits. Couldn't believe it when the bombs dropped, everything shaking. I asked if she wished to go below to the shelter. She said she didn't want to live, anyway. Then quite suddenly she said I had never loved her. That's simply — unfair, I cried — untrue. She didn't even listen to me. I could see smoke in the distance from the bombing and thought it might be as far away as Brighton. She said it no longer mattered, said she was already dead.

Then this look came into her face. I had never seen such a look before. Part leer, part wickedness, part cruelty. Olive was never cruel. Sharp, yes, but not cruel.

If you're not careful, she whispered, I may cut off your allowance altogether. Good God, woman, I shouted, you cannot mean that. I am already a bankrupt! If you were to withhold the allowance they would put me out on the street. Out on the street!

Then I thought, how odd! I have ended up exactly like Oscar did in his day. Both of us dependent upon the whim of unstable, estranged wives for a paltry monthly allowance. I do believe that should be the epitaph of each of us. Oscar and Bosie RIP. Punished by wives who wouldn't cough up. Circles, every-thing circling and circling back to everything else!

The door is thrown open behind him. A gigantic woman — wild, straggling red hair with several bald patches, wearing assorted clothing, marches in. She completely ignores DOUGLAS *who watches this apparition with astonishment. Weeping copiously, with the odd inarticulate groan and using a large cloth as handkerchief, she makes one or two rounds of the room, throwing her arms about in extravagant grief. Then, just as quickly, she sweeps out the door again.* DOUGLAS *closes it, nervously, behind her, shaking his head.*

(*Stage whisper*) That's Olive's Irish maid! Her name is Eil-eeen! Comes with the furniture, I'm afraid. Bit of a buffalo, what? For some extraordinary reason she doesn't seem aware that I'm actually present here. Very odd. She seems to be already engaged in some kind of Celtic wake. Does she think Olive's actually dead? Very odd.

Poor Olive! Why do we always end up fighting! Why? Even now. As she lies there, dying. One of our fearful rows. Started when I said, shouldn't Raymond be taken out from — (*difficulty*) from — dammit, man! Spit it out! St Andrew's Hospital for the Insane, Northampton! There! I've said it. My son is — a lunatic. She wouldn't hear of it. I said, for God's sake, Olive, he's our son! He should be here with you! I never wish to see him again, she screamed. No-no, you mustn't say that, dear, he's our boy. Don't care, she cried, hate him, hate him, tears streaming down her face, and I knew at once that what she was saying was that she hated me. In him. Poor Raymond! He's forty-two years old now, you know. Difficult to believe, isn't it? Forty-two!

Worse was to follow, I'm afraid. You see, what she's never been able to accept, Olive, is the damage her own father did to poor Raymond. Oh, yes, Colonel Frederic Custance, late of the Grenadiers. A sclerotic landed gent with a mouth full of rotten teeth. Knew how to land a salmon, though, the shit. Kidnapped his own grandson, would you believe! Can you believe that?

He had always wanted a son, Olive said. She spent her own childhood trying to be a boy, cutting her hair, building muscle, spitting and cursing and all the rest of it. Trying to impress Daddy. This whole business of sexual difference is greatly exaggerated, don't you think? *Ça va sans dire.*

Of course I blame Olive too. Despicable the way she behaved. When the chips were down she went over to Daddy's side. For over two years siding with the Colonel in his campaign against me. Against Raymond.

(*Distress, mimicry*) Want to be with Mamma and Grandad, Raymond screeched. Don't say that, Raymond! I want to be with Mamma and Grandad! Calm down, Raymond! Come and sit. There's a good chap!

Bosie, Mother called from another room, Bosie, take the boy to his mother and grandfather in Norfolk, he is wetting himself again! Want to be with Mamma and Grandad! No, Raymond, I said, I am your father. (*Fury*) Look at me, damn you, look me in the eye! He smelled of urine and perspiration and was holding some kind of blanket or towel or perhaps merely a fragment of cloth in both hands as if strangling something. Look me in the eye, Raymond! Bosie, Mother called and her voice appeared to come from a great distance — Bosie! — she called out in her best military manner — this is not a battle to be won! Her voice was like cannon

13

fire. Yield and retire! Re-group to fight another day! The boy is lost! Would have made a decent admiral, Mother. In her more heated moments she tended to say the same thing thrice. Each time the odds were shortened, somehow.

(*Slowly*) The boy is lost. Curious what happens when you mix blood with another. You produce something that is part of your flesh and blood and yet — not.

(*Eyes closed*) Such a beautiful child, playing on the grass at Aston Farm, Olive arched above him like a white bird, the Avon flowing steadily beyond them, all pulsing with life. I was so happy then, so happy. (*Eyes open*) But the truth is never beautiful like that. As I was to learn later. And as you shall see for yourselves, presently.

You see, what really got to Olive, what she simply couldn't take in — listen to this carefully — It's the first time it's been said publicly — her Daddy, the upright Colonel, conspired with a sodomite to corrupt my son. You don't believe me?

He grabs a bundle of papers, holding it up.

There! Proof! And who was this notorious bugger, you may ask, who aided and abetted the moral Colonel Custance, my delightful father-in-law? Who? Mr Robert Ross, that's who!

Yes, *that* Robert Ross! High Priest of the Wilde cult! Literary executor of Oscar Wilde, no less! The noble protector of the Wilde children! (*Mad rush*) Fat, balding Ross with that twaddle. Got him! Nailed him, I did! Hunted him out into the open. Showed him up for what he was, dirty little blackmailer, corruptor of — boys. Hundreds of boys! Pervert! (*Mincing sarcasm*) Always standing to one side at parties wearing that black silk skullcap, little finger raised above the rim of the glass, the scarab ring on display. Just so! Oh, don't mind me, don't pay any attention to little me! I'm just Robbie Ross, I'm merely the great defender of Oscar Wilde and all his works and pomps, the swine, miserable little Canadian bugger, by God, I swore I wouldn't rest until I had put him down.

(*Breathless stop, pulling himself together*) One thing he was never able to forget, Ross. Never! He might be Oscar's literary executor but I had been Oscar's — beloved. No contest.

Custance and Ross. Those two! In one year — what they did to my son, turned a bright boy full of sunshine into a blithering lunatic, staring in a corner, my boy Raymond, unable to talk to me. Ross and Custance. Sounds like a pair of bloody crooks up for embezzlement. No, sounds more like a pair of grocers. One year! Lost my wife. Lost my son. Declared bankrupt. Had to leave White's. Mustn't whinge. No whimpering, if you please. No sniffling. Stand up straight! Get it out into the open.

Very odd pairing, actually, Custance and Ross, when you think about it. I mean Squire Custance hated the very thought of queers while Robbie Ross was the queerest little madam in England.

You're simply paranoid, Olive yelled at me. How dare you speak of my father like that! I? Paranoid? Rubbish!

Look at all those court cases of yours, she cried. Well, it is true. I've been in court a few times. Well. Four or five times, can't remember, what has that got to do with it, I ask you? Well, it was thirteen or fourteen times in court, actually, if you must know.

Do you know, going to court is exactly like going to the races. People have this idea that it has to do with justice. Not in the least. It's all about winners and losers. Who stays coming into the home stretch, who nudges ahead at the post — I have the same rush of excitement before a jury as I have when my horse comes through the pack two furlongs out — do you happen to have the results from Kempton Park, by the way? No? I have a flutter in the 3.30. No, I don't suppose you do.

I had to go to court, had to, had to, all those damned libels. Ross putting about those lies that I deserted Wilde. I? Deserted? I who went with Oscar to Bow Street after his arrest? And what did Ross do? Scooted off to the boat train to Calais with half the queers in London. All the nervous nellies. Must have been like the beginning of the bloody Grand National, all tripping over one another, poor dears. Shouldn't wonder there was an orgy mid-channel, all hands on deck, so to speak.

One piece of advice, by the way, I always give people who go to court. Never throw away anything written on paper. Anything! That's how I beat off the Ross gang when they accused me of deserting Wilde. Produced my pass book. There in black and white. From the time he came out of prison to his death I gave Wilde over a thousand pounds. Not counting the money Mamma sent him.

And I paid for his funeral. Fact is, Wilde was utterly obsessed by two things. Money and titles. Irish, I suppose. He would finger the new notes from a moneylender with the same sensual pleasure with which he whispered in the ear of some sodden old duchess slumped in a chair.

I have never seen such terror on the face of another as on his when he heard that the cash had run out. Yet again. For God's sake, Oscar, it's only bloody money! You do not understand, Bosie, he would whisper, that large white face, absolute terror, staring at me as if I were his — murderer. Where did such fright come from, do you think? Are such fears planted in the womb?

What could the likes of Ross ever know about this? He was never an intimate of Oscar, never, more like a secretary or a butler. Whereas Oscar allowed me to see everything. Everything! He had this need, Oscar, to lower himself to the lowest. At first I couldn't understand it. For me it was just a bit of rough trade, like the sweaty haymakers at Bracknell when I was a boy. The tumble had the edge of — menace. You felt you were in the hands of someone who could conceivably — kill you. But that was it. Nothing one couldn't walk away from after a good scrub. Not Oscar, though. Oh, no.

Well, for one thing, I think he was incapable of accepting that service was something one paid for. Know what I mean? Pay up, move on. He couldn't do that, Oscar. There were always those dreadfully unclear moments at the end of all his trysts. It was as if he had some kind of affinity *au fond* with all those who served him, be they waiters or whores, always going on with this incredibly dangerous nonsense that one had to become whatever one desired.

Once, he was missing for two days. Didn't know that, did you? Two whole days! When I eventually found him I scarcely recognized this big, dishevelled brute with the stinking breath, the stubble, the filthy fingernails. Oscar? Is that you?

Had immense difficulty getting this cabby to take him on board even though that very same cabby knew him perfectly well for years as the elegant Mr Wilde. Took days to get him spick and span again.

He was simply grateful that I covered for him. He kissed my hands. How on earth could the likes of Ross ever understand such things?

Yes-Yes-Yes! I know I betrayed Wilde in court, I know it, no need to remind me for Heaven's sakes! Bloody law courts. Always say things in court one would never dream of saying elsewhere. Bit like bluffing at cards. Something gets into one in the dock. You get this overwhelming urge to — risk, to put everything on the red, to go beyond — safety.

Besides I was up before that blithering idiot, Mr Justice Darling. Yet again. I mean to say, that judicial clown has sat up before me on the bench in more cases —

Stops. A memory. A chuckle, then giggles.

Darling! Oh, dear God! I wrote him a letter once. (*More giggles*) Addressed him: My Dear Darling. They say he was unable to show his face in the club for weeks! (*Subsiding*) My Dear Darling. Oscar would have loved that.

He looks, puzzled, at the bundle of papers in his hands, takes out a pair of battered spectacles, reads.

Hello? What's all this, then? Mmm. Yes! Proof! This is the proof of everything I've just been saying! Custance and Ross, Ross and Custance.

I had employed a private detective, you see, a snoop, one Mr Littlechild. Littlechild — Littlechild, that name. It couldn't be! Impossible, surely!

You can't be the same Mr Littlechild! Same what, sir?

Same Mr Littlechild, the chap who dug up the dirt on Oscar Wilde for my father the Marquess of Queensberry? Donkey's years ago. You're far too young. Same family, sir. Family of Littlechilds. Well-well. All in the snoop business. Remarkable, I must say. I confess I looked at him a long while. In all his banality, in all his quite dreadful ordinariness, my sleuth, battered raincoat, the lot, my pimpled blood-hound carried something of the old figure of Fate.

What is it, sir? Nothing, I said, nothing. I was think-
ing, you see. Of Oscar.

What's this job then, sir? asked Mr Littlechild.
Well, Mr Littlechild, I said, producing photographs,
see these. I want you to follow this man, a Colonel
Custance, whenever he is accompanied by this boy,
showing a snap of Raymond. I must know where he
takes the boy, what they do together, and in particular I must know how the boy — whether or not he is
— happy. Do you follow?

Well, then. Listen to this! Not my words, mark
you! These are the words of Mr Littlechild from his
grubby notebook, more or less verbatim.

(*Reading*) Item. 'After tea, observed Colonel
Custance and Mr Ross on the footpath outside the
offices of Lewis and Lewis, Solicitors. At first both
men seemed to be in a bit of a tiff over something.
Then all was good cheer. They walked away together,
laughing over something, and the Colonel clapped
Mr Ross on the back.'

Item. 'Followed Colonel Custance and the boy
Raymond into Simpsons. The Colonel bought something for the boy. When they came out Mr Ross had
joined them. Job had to be abandoned over danger
of discovery by the subjects.'

Item. 'Followed the boy Raymond to the National
Portrait Gallery. The boy Raymond was met by Mr
Ross at the entrance. The boy was taken into gallery
by Mr Ross and afterwards to tea at the Savoy.' Tea at
the Savoy! My son! That monster Custance delivered
my son — my son! — into the hands of that filthy
little queen, Ross! Unspeakable! Of all the — Allowing
my son to be, to be, to be — entertained — in the
hands of — (*shaking with rage*)

Mustn't go that way, mustn't, mustn't! (*Rapidly*)
O Sacred Heart of Jesus I place all my trust in Thee!
O Sacred Heart of Jesus place all my trust! O Sacred

Heart of Jesus I place all my — (*He blesses himself, eyes closed for a moment*)

That's better. Thank you, Jesus. Thank you.

But I tell you this! He had not been sick before that encounter, Raymond. I swear it! That is why I destroyed the remains of the Wilde cult. Ross is dead! I have come into the light and left behind the places of iniquity! I have been saved from my past life and left behind the sins of my youth!

(*Quick change in tone*) Had this thought the other day. I am haunted by children. No. Rather — child, yes, haunted by the child. The impossible promise of that innocence untouched. Oh, Raymond! That's why I'm looking forward to Heaven, by the way. In Heaven one can be absolutely anything one wishes. I intend to be a child. Forever.

A loud banging of a stick upon the floor from above. He looks up.

That's Olive! She's got this walking stick beside the bed. Thump! Thump! (*Towards door*) Have to go up to her, I'm afraid. (*Calling out*) Coming, Olive! Sorry about that, must go. (*Heading out the door, he turns to audience*) Back in a jiffy!

He goes off. Music. Lights down. Bell tolling in distance. Brief pause.

Lights up. Daylight. Strong contrast of bright sunshine from the window which picks out the blue colours of the room. DOUGLAS *enters in a smart grey suit, black tie, polished shoes, carrying a bunch of lilies. He immediately goes to the window and looks off into the sunlight.*

(*Turning to audience*) Suppose you've heard the news? Olive. Died three days ago. February 12th, 1944. Won't forget that date. You know, when I became a Catholic she followed me to Rome. Much to the fury of her Daddy the Colonel who hated everything Roman, particularly priests. Then, before the end, she lapsed. What terrifies me now is that I may never see her again. I mean — in the hereafter.

(*Eyes closed*) O Merciful God, take the immortal soul of Olive Custance into Thy bosom for all eternity. Amen.

(*To window*) She wants her ashes scattered out here. At sea, in the Channel. What a dreadful prospect. She howled and howled at the end, what was left of her shaking, her small body so brittle. Then, in a most composed voice, she said, I am going into the garden with Raymond. That's the last coherent thing she said to me. If you can call that coherent. Going into the garden with Raymond. Imagine!

(*Sudden, forced animation*) He's here, you know! Raymond! Yes! This very moment. They allowed him out for the funeral, scattering of ashes, perhaps tomorrow. He's upstairs in one of the bedrooms. Of course he's got to rest. We mustn't disturb him, now. The people at the — at the — the — asylum, rest and quiet, they said, he will need rest and quiet after his mother's — actually, I don't think he knows what the hell is going on. Would be terrified to have my ashes scattered at sea, absolutely terrified. Wouldn't you?

(*Looks up above, anxiously*) Just a moment! Did you hear something? Raymond? (*A hand up*) Shush! No? Thought I heard a board — creaking, door, maybe? Perhaps he's moving about? No, nothing.

(*Forced*) He's perfectly fine now, Raymond is. Tremendously recovered. Tip-top spirits. You would never think he was — well, you know what I mean

21

— well, I suppose, I should warn you before you meet him for the first time. He can be a trifle — boisterous — at first. Overdoing the handshake. That kind of thing. But don't be nervous. He's simply a — hearty boy. Likes jokes. But perfectly fine, now, perfectly normal again. Normal —

(*Reflects*) I think Olive and I would have been fine together if we had never married. We could have been like brother and sister. There are relationships like that, you know. Just pottering about together. Never lonely.

Bloody awful business, marriage. It seems to test everything to the limit. Especially sex. I've been chaste now for thirty years and it's done me a world of good. No wonder the monasteries and convents are full of healthy oldies.

What I mean is that Olive and I were attracted to each other's sexual shadow, she to my feminine side and I to her masculine. I understand it now. Too late, yes, I know, I know.

At any rate, there I was, 1901, standing about, mooning over her, an apparition with her curls tucked away under a jaunty yachting cap, thumbs stuck in the waistband of her white slacks, hip jutting out like a young buck. I called her my page, she called me her boy-girl. Marriage soon put a stop to that tommyrot, I can tell you.

Or, more accurately, *it* put a stop to the marriage. What a flirt she was! While I was busily trying to be manly. Exactly what she didn't want. What she wanted of me was something — sexually ambiguous. While I was desperately seeking — sexual definition for myself. Impossible odds, don't you think? What a sexual zoo it all is, when you think about it!

(*Outburst of anger*) She hated Raymond! How she hated him! Hated giving birth to him, hated watching him become — seeing him sink into — madness.

He is yours, she yelled at me. Take him! He's not mine! I can never forgive her for that! Never! I tried to be a mother and father to Raymond. How could I be? The boy suffered. Confused. Mother and father to him, indeed. I let her have her fling.

What an appallingly vulgar word that is, by the way. Fling! Still, it does have a certain — ring to it.

She even consorted once with an Irish bishop at a boxing match. An Irish bishop! I ask you! Let her, I said, to anyone who would listen. It is a matter of indifference to me. (*It clearly isn't. Pause. Looks off*)

Never really liked the sea. Something to be crossed. En route. As expeditiously as possible. All that damn liquid. Drowning. What a way to go. Prefer to die in bed.

It is extraordinary how easily I am taken in! I believe in God despite all evidence to the contrary. I believe in moral courage, people being decent to one another to get one through the day while the whole bloody world is going to the dogs. The important thing, as dear Mother used to say, is to be constantly on guard. Never hope for too much, darling, that's what she would say, as I departed after a visit to her flat. Just up the road here in Hove, her flat. Keep on the look-out, Bosie, she would call from her favourite armchair. Hadn't a bean at the end, poor old Mother. I could hear her voice from the front door, booming out. (*Calling out, hand to mouth*) Beware the unexpected, darling!

The door suddenly bursts open behind him so that he jumps in alarm to one side. ELEEN bursts in, carrying a large, laden tray, tea things and plates piled high with buns and cake. She knocks over items of furniture in transit as she throws down the tray on the table. She pays no attention whatsoever to DOUGLAS who quakes to one side.

Good God, it's she again! (*Calling out*) Do be careful, there's a dear! Careful now! Mind that vase! Oh, my God, look at that!

EILEEN *clumps out as she came in, leaving the door open.* DOUGLAS *tentatively approaches the door and peeps out after her. Pauses. Closes door, nervous, relieved.*

Gone! Won't see her again in a hurry, thank goodness. (*Turns to table*) Aha! The tea! We make the tea each day at this time. I mean Eileen does. Just in case some of the young chaps drop by to visit me. Hugh or Malcolm or that chap Croft-Cooke.

I must say she does make the most scrumptious buns and tarts, old Eileen, whatever else. How on earth she gets everything on the ration books is beyond me. Never know there was a war on, would you? Could there be some kind of Irish black market in the back streets of Hove, do you think? How unlikely! Goes to the bookies for me, too, the dear. Have to write out the bets for her on a bit of paper. They know her by now down at the corner. Thirty-seven pounds ten shillings the other day on a two-bob double, not bad, eh? Gave Eileen one-and-sixpence out of the proceeds. She went off and spent it on Woodbines. Smokes like a chimney.

Maybe young Adrian or young Richard with his pals will drop by? Or that nice young Donald Sinden who wishes to be an actor.

Love to listen to their boyish chatter. Makes me feel — young again, watching them scoffing Eileen's buns. Just like school again. She hides somewhere while they are here. I do believe she's afraid to show herself to the boys. Poor thing. She's quite sensitive, actually, underneath that agricultural exterior.

I should say, though, that she's frightfully good

with Raymond. Tremendously caring. What I mean is I'm too old, now, to — He's very strong, you know, surprisingly strong for someone who — very difficult to — hold down. Middle-aged man, now, hard to believe. (*He looks up above, listening*) I wonder if he's sleeping —

(*Breaks, great distress*) Why don't I just tell the truth for once! Oh, dear God, the whole thing is dreadful, dreadful! She just seizes him, Eileen, and throws him down on the bed, and he is utterly submissive to her. I stand there at the bedroom door, watching them, unable to move, unable to say a word. It's like an appalling wrestling match. She always wins, old Eileen. My poor boy. My son.

(*Looks at table*) Someone is bound to drop by, don't you think? (*Looks at watch*) Maybe later. What do we talk about, you ask? Mostly me, I'm afraid.

They are utterly thrilled that Oscar and I ended up in gaol. Different times, of course. And different — I almost said crimes! I told the boys that I had played the harmonium for Benediction with the prison choir in Wormwood Scrubs. Never heard such perfect notation from the hymnal, especially from a group of Sinn Féiners, no less, in for political outrages. Glorious voices, would you believe. Never know, do you? Singing gunmen!

Point is, I couldn't bring myself to tell the boys what prison had done to me. How it forced truth on me so that I cannot look on myself any more without terror at what monstrous things I have been capable of in my life.

Then, one day, one of the boys, young Richard, dawdled behind after the others had gone. Yes? I asked him. Can I help? He hummed and hawed and clearly had great difficulty in getting it out. Why, he asked eventually, why had Oscar Wilde written that terrible letter about me when he was in prison when he and I clearly loved one another to the end? Oh, innocence! Innocence! I found the look on the boy's face unbearable.

He wanted some answer but was terrified that the answer would destroy some belief which he held dear. Come along, I said, come back in, and back the two of us came to what remained of Eileen's tea and buns.

He sat there. (*Pointing*) Right there, expectantly waiting. I said to him, I shall tell you, I shall tell you why Wilde wrote that horrible letter about me. And why I was able to forgive him. The truth was, however, that I hadn't an earthly idea of what to say next. We looked dumbly at one another for a minute or two. Awful!

Then this most curious thing happened. (*Looking up*) Raymond came into my mind. Raymond, in all the wreckage of his mind and body! And I knew, at once, what it was that I had to say to the boy. I told him that prison was about failure. No-no-no, I do not mean that one is put in the clink because one has failed at this or that, no, I mean something else. In prison, if one is fortunate, that is, one meets total and absolute human failure. One meets it like a familiar presence. It is there, palpable and immovable like another person in the cell.

The young lad hadn't a notion of what I was trying to say. He looked at me and I grieved at his innocent puzzlement, but what could I do about it? He couldn't see that I was telling him an essential truth about human existence.

That at the very heart of existence is this well of failure and that to look into this black pool is to cleanse oneself, forever, of all illusion, about others, about oneself. How could I explain that Oscar, too, had looked into this pit and then wrote that terrible letter about me? How could I explain that that was the reason, too, why I could forgive him? You see, we had both become truth-tellers, able to cut through deception, especially our own self-deception.

On that note, I have to confess to you now that I've been lying to you. Yes! Most of what I've been saying to you — a pack of lies! About Raymond. I mean about Ross and Custance and Raymond. All lies, simply to make me feel better about myself. What a shit I am!

Unsteadily he gets to his knees in the mode of prayer. Joins his hands, eyes closed.

All merciful God! I pray for my enemies. I pray for the salvation of the immortal soul of my father-in-law, Frederic Hambledon Custance. I pray for the repose of the soul of Robert Baldwin Ross who sought to destroy me. Custance and Ross. Ross and Custance. I confess to Almighty God that I have — lied about my enemies, Ross and Custance, whom I yoked together because I was unable to face the truth about my son, my own flesh and blood!

They never belonged together, Custance and Ross, except in my mad lying. They had no part in the sickness of my son, Raymond. Raymond's madness is of my own flesh and blood. He is in me and I am in him. This thing of darkness I acknowledge mine! Amen.

He climbs painfully to his feet once more, much sighing.

You know that doesn't make me feel the slightest bit better. Quite the contrary. What a pair of skunks they were, those two, Custance and Ross. What is it about me that all my life I've attracted the attention of absolute shits?

Olive said her Daddy died cursing me. Nice, very nice, I must say. Of course he failed, old Custance, in the one thing he desired. He lost Raymond, despite all his machinations.

Now, Ross was a different kettle of fish. Oho! A fine specimen of sodomitical treachery, Ross. Listen to this! For twelve years after Oscar's death, twelve years! — this — this maggot — this rotten little twerp, went about pretending to be a friend of mine — this Judas in the black skullcap. What a rotter he was! All those years having in his possession — unknown to me — those letters of Oscar's and mine. Feeding them into courtroom after courtroom — courtcase after courtcase — (*shaking with emotion, a moment to recover*)

Allow me to tell you my final story of Ross. Oscar had died in Paris. Winter of the year 1900. Nearly fifty years ago now! I had travelled as quickly as I could to Paris from Scotland. I stood in that ugly little room in the Hotel d'Alsace with Ross above Oscar's closed coffin. Which I had paid for, incidentally. Then Ross said to me, we have had to nail down the lid before your arrival. I asked why. He wouldn't or couldn't answer so I yelled at him, Speak up, man, damn you! Why cannot I see Oscar's face? I was perfectly prepared for anything. It did not matter to me how he looked. I had thought of nothing else on that hectic journey across England and the Channel but of looking on his face one last time.

What is it, Ross? I demanded. Why cannot I see Oscar's face? He snuffled into a handkerchief, cambric in the air, his face turned away from me. I found all this positively old-maidish. Eventually he turned and whispered to me, (*imitation whisper*) the body has already begun to decompose.

This was bad enough but more was to follow. I

stood above the coffin shaking with terror and grief so that I barely heard the next words that came from Ross. To compound matters he spoke in a low voice.

There are papers, he whispered, letters and such like. Do you wish to look at them? (*Outburst*) What? What? I roared. What? What?

Then he whispered yet again, I will deal with them. If you wish. (*Outburst*) Oh, deal with them, deal with them, Ross, and simply leave me alone, damn you!

I wished to grieve, you see, in private. With Oscar.

So he left the room, Ross, taking my lifeblood with him, although I did not know it at the time. He was carrying the letters with which I was persecuted in courtroom after courtroom, until his death. He was carrying that horrible letter that Oscar had written about me to be produced in court twelve years later. Twelve years! The little sneak had hidden it away, a letter addressed to me. For God's sake, the fellow believed it was *his* letter! He even gave it the name *De Profundis*! The nerve of the scoundrel!

Oh, my God, I mustn't go on like this! Must not! Must not! Turn me into a monster again. Please God, help me to control myself. Mustn't think about Ross. Ever again. All that is — finished. Think of the crucified Christ. Think of the Child Jesus. In the cell.

Oscar said he saw Christ in the cell, you know. Can't talk about that with my young visitors. Couldn't bear the thought of their — sniggering at that.

Actually, I had trouble believing Oscar when he first told me. He said that, in the foul morning light of the cell, this — this figure would come and stand in the corner. The tortured saviour, the white, bruised flesh shading into blue and black. Like one of those over-ripe Spanish statues, Oscar would say, but — breathing.

I think I found the whole thing preposterous until

— until — I have difficulty in saying this! Well — out with it, for Heaven's sakes! Get it out, man! (*Deep breath*) Very well. I know you will have difficulty believing this. The same thing happened to me twenty-five years later in my cell at Wormwood Scrubs. There! I've said it, finally! Never mentioned a word of this to anyone before. Not even Olive.

Christ came to me, too, in the cell. It was not the battered Christus of Golgotha. No. It was the twelve-year-old boy, waxing strong in spirit, who had tarried behind in Jerusalem at Passover, making his parents frantic at his disappearance. It was the twelve-year-old boy who astonished the doctors of the Temple with his understanding, a boy of radiant face and uplifted finger, a boy the colour of fine sand, and although all was silent in my wretched cell I knew immediately, and in full, the message of the boy to the elders that day in the Temple in Jerusalem. (*A kind of chant*) It was that innocence is not of this world. That innocence is a brief flare of light from beyond. That innocence cannot last beyond the morning dew. That innocence beguiles us because it cannot be possessed.

(*Shift*) Very odd thing, physical beauty. It can be like a deformity, you know, a sort of blight. You mightn't think it now, to look at me, but I suffered that myself when I was young. Innocence. Once we try to possess innocence, then all is — destruction! Yes, I was beautiful — once. Means nothing now.

The loud crash of a falling body from above. DOUGLAS *jumps and looks up. Silence. He whispers the name*

Raymond! Raymond.

Then, head down, he begins to pace back and forth,

back and forth, from side to side of the stage. He stops. Looks up. Still silence. He goes, opens the door, but is unable to go out. Comes back, stands anxiously, looking up, as if knowing exactly what is to happen next. At once the noise starts up again. A body crashing into furniture, falling, kicking and punching the floor, heels pounding, heavy panting, gasping. DOUGLAS *rushes to the door, yelling*

Eileen! Eileen! Go up to him! Quickly! Quickly!

Sounds of things being thrown about above, sounds of heavy feet clumping up the stairs. DOUGLAS *at the open door, shouting*

Be — be gentle with him! Oh, please be gentle!

He comes back in again, stricken, shaking.

I cannot go up there, cannot! Cannot! Cannot! My boy, my only son!

He tries to shut out everything, hands to ears, moaning to himself, head shaking from side to side.
A final noise from above as of two bodies struggling, then a body thrown down upon a bed, bedsprings shaking, then inarticulate, gasping, hissing sounds. Then silence. DOUGLAS *registers the silence. Then goes and slowly closes the door.*

More lies! I lied when I said he was — fine. He is anything but well. Is most dreadfully ill, in fact. The only question is who will suffer his violence? He himself? Or another? The truth is I am afraid of my own son. Terrified of him. Isn't that the most dreadful thing to have to say. Lies! Lies! Always the same futile effort to avoid facing — what is! Incurable, that's what they said, the team of doctors in suits behind the table in Northampton. Incurable!

He goes and opens the door, nervously, and calls in a low voice

Eileen? Eileen? Are you there?

No answer, which is a kind of relief to him. He now sits, or rather collapses, on a chair.

The thing is I have always known, well almost always, something eating him away. Tried to ignore it. As was my wont then.

One day — he would have been no more than — what? — four? Five? I stood in the bay window at Aston Farm, the summer boiling away outside the window, the trees heavy with heat and growth, the garden raging in colour and beyond, the river — Shakespeare's river, moving slowly down into the heart of England, the water like heavy, molten metal between the greenery.

Olive had her back to me about fifty, no, forty yards from where I stood behind the glass, oh, what the hell does it matter? Distance — Quite near, at any rate, making what happened next particularly difficult to understand — I mean, why did I not stop it at once? She was a lithe, white figure in a hat, with a yellow basket, bent over some flowery activity, no, not weeding, she loathed weeding, Olive, but leaning in over the bed, that long back, those delicate hips. She was a slight movement in the haze.

He stops again for a moment, the lips moving silently, as if recalling her from the dead. Then he pulls himself together once more.

(*Sudden harshness*) Raymond! (*Stops himself. More calmly*) Raymond was playing on the grass some little distance from her and four or five feet further away from where I stood. Everything was placed with a kind of precision. My wife. My son. And I behind the glass. A necessary precision before some gross violation.

(*A shudder, then more gently*) Raymond's back was to her back, a small, dumpy garden elf, dressed in plaid jacket and knickerbockers which were all the rage that summer for young mothers and their sunburnt offspring. Yankee influence, I do believe.

Got to be careful with the next bit. Got to get it right. What I mean is that although I remember the domestic peace of the moment, at the same time I know I felt extremely troubled at the sight. I remember narrowing my focus to concentrate upon the child in the blinding summer sun, fearful that I might lose sight of him. What was troubling was that I knew that such concentration was not — love.

(*Pause, seeing each detail*) Raymond suddenly, unsteadily, clambered to his feet. And turned.

(*Deep distress*) I shall never forget the look on that child's face because it is the same look on the face of that fortytwo-year-old man in that bed upstairs! It is the look of the animal on the human face! Inflated cheeks and small eyes lost in the swollen flesh. Mouth like a rodent. Sniff! Sniff! Sniff! This feral child moved. It waddled forward, hunting head thrust out for prey. I tried to open the window, I banged upon it, but to my horror this had no effect whatsoever, as if I were pounding silk.

My wife lay across the coverlet of flowers like a sacrifice.

I tried calling out, of course I did! Wouldn't you? But she couldn't hear me in my glass jar of silence, sweat pouring down my body inside my clothing, a smell like ordure in the stifling air.

I was trying to call, Olive! Olive! but was baffled as to whether it was a warning or some inexplicable reminder to her of something she already knew. The rat-boy advanced through the grass as through his familiar element. With a kind of careless acceptance of what was convenient to him he lifted up an open, pronged shears and lunged at his mother's vulnerable back.

The memory is almost too much for him. He stands, shaking. Then he straightens up again with fierce composure.

Something released me and I raced from the room. It would have taken me no more than ten or twenty seconds to reach the kitchen and the kitchen door, five to round the side of the house and enter the garden gate with its mantle of wisteria.

There I ran into Olive, carrying the sleeping child in her arms, his arms and legs loosened in perfect peace, his face lost in her shoulder. I sobbed and grasped her free arm. What on earth is the matter, darling? she cried. You look frightful!

He staggers to the door. Opens it, listens. Closes the door and returns.

How quiet it is now! Perhaps he is sleeping? With that Irish giantess standing guard at the foot of his bed, watching over him like some primeval mother.

(*Looking at tea things*) Don't suppose anyone is going to come today. Perhaps tomorrow? Or the next day? Richard, or young Donald with his backstage gossip. No. No one is going to come for Eileen's tea.

If only Raymond had had proper young friends like those! Never was able to make proper friends.

Liked grooms and gillies. Always got on terrifically well with waiters and waitresses. Did I tell you about that young woman who tried to marry him? No? Some story. What was her name? Doris? Daisy? Can't remember. Awful! (*Listens at door again*) He's quiet now. I think we do not have to —

Oh, my family! The Douglas line! I keep having this — flash — like something suddenly lit up — like memory but not memory because I have this strong sense of it belonging to the future, yes, my own future, beyond the grave.

A line of dim figures out of a mist, upon the Highland moors, some blood-boltered, some with bloodstained hands, some hacked with the most grievous wounds and, then, unmistakably in this stygian parade, a place waiting for myself. (*Pause*) And a place for Raymond!

Oh, Raymond! Marriage to that girl would have made no difference. Absolutely not. Wouldn't have made him better. Utterly unsuitable, she was. Daisy? What the devil was her name? Name reminded me of — tea-shops. Or the seaside, for some damned reason. My mind's gone, with everything else.

We were in Nice, he and I, must have been '26, '27? One morning he had gone out and something moved me, a — premonition, to step out after him.

As I turned into the Promenade des Anglais, there he stood! In that curious crouching position that he has when his full attention is caught, on a trout, perhaps, or a grouse, or, as in this particular case, a floosie in a floral dress, swinging her handbag in front of him, like a lure, or, indeed, a thurible, at any rate, an offering in his face. His eyes, his great, big dark eyes were on the swinging handbag but I could also see that he was chattering away good-oh to this flirt, as was his wont, indeed, ever the garrulous Raymond, no matter who was in front of him, now this pert madam with her handbag.

Among other things I was put in mind of the bull-ring, a female toreador, goading the animal to charge.

After lunch I nailed him. By the by, Raymond, who was that young lady you were speaking with just now on the street? Oh, she's frightfully well-born, Father. As soon as I heard this I knew at once that we were on the bottom rung of the ladder. Odd thing is that I first thought, so what? Let the boy have — his fling, if only — once.

My good wife and my darling mother soon put a stop to that particular aspiration. Bosie!, Mother cried, you are placing the boy in the gutter! He will end up in the stews! Have you ascertained this young lady's credentials?

Olive answered that one in double-quick time. Olive dug out the dirt. The young lady's name was Gladys! There, I've remembered it, Gladys! Seaside, strand and tea-rooms with bunting. Her Daddy a grocer in Shropshire, now deceased, her Mummy running the local pub.

Raymond wept. I held him in my arms, a mother and father to him, indeed. He has lied to us, Olive cried, lied about her age. Her origins. She is a trollop, Olive screamed, she's been living with the same man for years! Raymond weeping was like a four-year-old again, great, oily tears, gripping my shoulder, heaving and snuffling exactly as when he had a grazed knee and I put on the iodine.

What did we kill in him, Olive, Mother and I, when we forbade him to see his Gladys? That is the only question worth asking anymore. What was it that died in him?

A sudden, piercing male scream from above. It lasts for several seconds, dying away into gasping and panting. Then silence. DOUGLAS *remains rivetted by this, standing and facing the audience. When the sound has ended he whispers*

Raymond.

He turns and slowly goes to the door, opens it, listens, closes the door and comes back down again.

He is calling to me, Raymond, from inside his madness. Calling to me from the garden of chaos. I must go to him. He has no one else, you see. I am his mother and father. No one else. (*Calling*) Coming, Raymond!

The sound, from above, of a body being roughly handled, heels dragged on the floor, a bumping into furniture. DOUGLAS *stops and listens to this.*

My God, what is she doing up there? (*Yells*) Hello! Bring him down here! Eileen? Can you hear me?

The sound of heavy footsteps descending the stairs.

Poor Raymond — calling to me. We're going to take our places, you know, he and I! Yes, in that dim line of figures on the darkened moor, the bloodied family of Douglas, all violence come to an end.

DOUGLAS *does not move but he listens as the steps descend. They stop outside the door. The door is kicked open.*

    EILEEN *stands there holding the limp figure of* RAYMOND *in her arms, his legs and arms hanging down, his head turned away, out of sight, on her shoulder. She puts him down and he leans into her, unable to stand on his own.*

    DOUGLAS *turns to face them in the doorway.*

EILEEN *holds* RAYMOND *up and she helps him as they move off, out of sight.* DOUGLAS *follows them out through the open doorway and the play ends.*